Original title:
The Deep Ocean

Copyright © 2024 Swan Charm Publishing
All rights reserved.

Editor: Jessica Elisabeth Luik
Author: Leena Meripõld
ISBN HARDBACK: 978-9916-86-018-2
ISBN PAPERBACK: 978-9916-86-019-9

Darkwater Dreams

In the quiet depths where shadows play,
Lies the realm where night meets day.
Silence whispers to the cold,
Stories of secrets left untold.

Moonlight dances on the waves,
Guiding souls to hidden caves.
Mariners drift on endless streams,
Lost within their darkwater dreams.

Whales echo ancient songs,
In the depths where time belongs.
Currents weave a mystic seam,
Binding all in darkwater dreams.

Coastline Shadows

Beneath the cliffs where seagulls cry,
Shadows stretch beneath the sky.
Waves wash secrets on the shore,
Echoes of the days before.

Sunsets paint the evening gold,
Stories of the coast retold.
Whispers in the twilight breeze,
Ghostly footprints in the seas.

Night descends with velvet cloak,
Stars awaken, dreams invoke.
Coastline shadows softly gleam,
Merging with the ocean's theme.

Luminous Deep

In the ocean's sapphire kiss,
Lies a realm of pure abyss.
Glowing creatures, light as beams,
Dance within the luminous deep.

Plankton sparkles, waves alight,
Guiding us through velvet night.
Silent beauty, secrets keep,
Hushed within the ocean's deep.

Anemones in colors bloom,
Bright against the water's gloom.
Life that in the depths does leap,
Awes us with the luminous deep.

Horizon's Depth

Where the sky meets endless blue,
Dreams of distant lands come true.
Ships sail on to worlds unknown,
Chasing where horizons roam.

Golden rays of dawn's first light,
Chase away the cloak of night.
Promises the sun has kept,
Guide us to horizon's depth.

Stars watch silently in sleep,
O'er the secrets oceans keep.
In the vast expanse, we're swept,
Mesmerized by horizon's depth.

Phantom Light Below

In shadowed depths, a glimmer bright,
Eternal whispers, a silent plight.
Where currents weave their ancient lore,
A phantom light shines evermore.

Beneath the waves, a somber hue,
The deep reveals a world askew.
Within the dark, a dreamy glow,
Phantom light doth ebb and flow.

Mysterious gleam in ocean's embrace,
It dances with grace, leaves no trace.
Haunting depths where secrets keep,
Phantom light, forever deep.

Serenade of the Abyss

In the heart of ocean wide,
Where shadows and mysteries abide.
A lullaby in gentle wakes,
A serenade the abyss makes.

Softly hums the ancient sea,
A song of timeless mystery.
Beneath the surface, calm and deep,
Where dreams and secrets gently seep.

Echoes of a distant time,
In watery realms so sublime.
A serenade of silent bliss,
Whispered by the abyss.

Tranquil Submersion

Below the waves, in calm repose,
Where liquid peace in currents flows.
A tranquil world of quiet dreams,
Bathed in soft aquatic gleams.

Serenity in ocean's heart,
A silent realm where troubles part.
In stillness of the blue profound,
Tranquil submersion doth surround.

Immersed in waters silent sway,
Time stands still, night or day.
In depths where tranquil whispers sing,
Peaceful submersion in ocean's ring.

Rise of the Abyssal Mysteries

From the deep where shadows reside,
Rise the secrets, far and wide.
Mysteries of the abyss unfold,
Tales forgotten, legends told.

Woken from their silent sleep,
Ancient truths begin to seep.
Whispers from the abyssal night,
Reveal their secrets, dark and bright.

Rise they do from depths below,
Mysteries with a spectral glow.
Abyssal wonders, bound in lore,
Awaken now, forever more.

Chasm of Secrets

A whisper in the void, lost but not forgotten,
Echoes of the past, deep and begotten,
Mysteries linger, like shadows unseen,
In the chasm of secrets, where dreams convene.

Stars flicker softly, like ancient lore,
Guardians of truth, forevermore,
In that silent expanse, so vast and wide,
Lies the chasm of secrets, where enigmas reside.

Every heartbeat, a silent vow,
To unveil the unknown, to lift the shroud,
Yet in the depth, where darkness prevails,
The chasm of secrets, tenderly exhales.

A dance of shadows, a waltz of night,
Guided by whispers, hidden from sight,
In every crevice, a story untold,
The chasm of secrets, timeless and bold.

Eternal Abyss

Deep within the abyss, where silence reigns,
Eternal and boundless, free of chains,
Stars gaze down from their lofty height,
Lighting the abyss, in a celestial fight.

Whispers of the past, and dreams that scream,
In the eternal abyss, where shadows teem,
Infinity cradles the hopes and cries,
Of every soul, beneath the skies.

The eternal abyss, where lost souls wander,
In search of meaning, they seldom ponder,
Endless expanse, a void so grand,
Swallowing moments, like grains of sand.

A symphony of darkness, a silent choir,
The eternal abyss, its depths inspire,
Every heartbeat, a call to the unknown,
In the void of eternity, we're never alone.

Enshrouded Blue

The sky enshrouded in deepest blue,
As twilight's veil descends anew,
Stars emerge from velvet night,
Glinting with celestial might.

Whispers of the evening breeze,
Dance among the silent trees,
Moonbeams cast their gentle light,
Chasing shadows out of sight.

Oceans hum their lullaby,
Beneath the tranquil, starry sky,
Tides caress the sandy shore,
As day departs forevermore.

Marine Shadows

Beneath the waves of deep abyss,
Lies a realm of silent bliss,
Creatures of the darkest hue,
In shadows hide from searching view.

Coral forests, colors bright,
In twilight's grasp, lose their light,
Fleeting glimmers, scales aglow,
In the depths, their secrets show.

Midnight currents softly sway,
Drawing night into the day,
Marine shadows come to play,
In the ocean's grand ballet.

Currents of Night

Midnight currents weave and wind,
Through the ocean, undefined,
Waves that whisper tales untold,
Of treasures deep and ages old.

Stars reflect on waters vast,
Eons merge, the future, past,
Moonlit pathways guide the way,
In the depths where shadows play.

Silent echoes, soft and clear,
From the depths bring stories near,
Currents of the night untamed,
By the sea shall be reclaimed.

Below the Foam

Beneath the foam, in hidden lair,
Life unfolds with quiet care,
Silent worlds that drift and weave,
In the currents, hearts believe.

Colors blend in depths unknown,
Life persists, unseen, alone,
Mysteries of the ocean sway,
In the dusk at end of day.

Quiet echoes, whispers faint,
Songs the waters softly paint,
Below the foam in twilight's dome,
Lies a world that calls us home.

Black Sea Mystery

In the depths of blackened sea,
Where shadows twist and twine,
Lies a mystery to be,
Where dark and stars align.

Whispers from the silent deep,
Hold tales of lost despair,
Secrets that the currents keep,
In an endless, murky lair.

Moonlight glints on waters dark,
Guiding souls who drift away,
Every wave a cryptic mark,
Where night consumes the day.

Ancient echoes softly stray,
Through the heavy, somber gloom,
Drawing wanderers astray,
To meet their silent doom.

In the depths of blackened sea,
Where shadows twist and twine,
A deeper truth yearns to be,
Forever left behind.

Marine Tranquility

Gentle waves kiss sandy shores,
Whispering tales of olden days,
Peaceful breezes sift and soar,
In the light of sunset's rays.

Silence wraps the ocean blue,
A quilt of calm tranquility,
Sweeping skies in pastel hue,
Embrace the sea's serenity.

Seagulls drift in lazy dance,
Above the tranquil, glassy sea,
Nature's lullaby enchants,
In a melody of glee.

Stars reflect in water's face,
A canvas pure and wide,
Time and space embrace in grace,
In the ocean's gentle tide.

Beneath the moon's soft silver beam,
The sea whispers, soft and free,
Eternal peace in every dream,
Of marine tranquility.

Below the Crest

Beneath the ocean's rolling crest,
Lies a world of silent lore,
Hidden treasures long at rest,
Lie upon the sandy floor.

Coral castles, bright and fair,
Hold secrets of the past,
Fish in colors vivid, rare,
In shadows they do cast.

Waves above may rage and swell,
But peace resides below,
In the deep, a tranquil spell,
Where time moves ever slow.

Dark and light in balance find,
Harmony beneath the sea,
Life unfurls in every kind,
In coral caves, wild and free.

Beneath the ocean's rolling crest,
Mysteries deep and profound,
In the waters, souls find rest,
In the sea's embrace, they're bound.

Azure Abyss

In the abyss, so deep and blue,
Life resides in realms unseen,
Shadows dance in twilight's hue,
Where the ocean's heart has been.

Creatures glide in silent grace,
Through the depths of endless night,
In the dark they leave no trace,
Hidden far from surface light.

Anemones in colors bright,
Wave like banners in the sea,
Bioluminescent light,
Guides them through their mystery.

In the silence, time suspends,
Drifting softly in the deep,
Where the ocean's story blends,
With the dreams we softly keep.

In the abyss, so deep and blue,
Secrets of the past persist,
Unraveled in the cosmic view,
Of the endless azure abyss.

Blue Abyss Odyssey

Into the abyss, I boldly steer
Mysterious depths, I hold no fear
A world concealed in sapphire waves
With ancient tales that darkness saves

Creatures glide in shadowed ballet
Their silent song, a hidden play
Through coral mazes, I drift and weave
In the blue abyss, I believe

Each ripple whispers secrets old
Of sunken ships and treasures cold
In endless night, the journey calls
A boundless quest, where courage falls

Silent Seafloor

Beneath the waves, where light can't reach
A world obscured, without speech
The seafloor lies in spectral peace
Its mysteries never to cease

Crustaceans crawl in muted march
Across the sand, beneath an arch
Rustling echoes softly fade
In the silent seafloor's serene parade

Anemones dance with gentle grace
In this tranquil, hidden place
Time moves slow, a tender sway
In the seafloor's hush, we stay

Submersible Soliloquy

Alone I plunge, in vessel's womb
To ocean's depths, escaping gloom
A soliloquy of steel and light
To chart a course in endless night

Lights ablaze, through dark we cut
The silence, deep, a lonely strut
In pressure's grasp, the hull does creak
Yet through it all, no word I speak

Exploring worlds that time forgot
In quietude, I find my lot
The ocean's heart, my soul's reprieve
In metal shell, I do believe

Inky Veil Dawn

The dawn peeks beyond the inky veil
As shadows stretch and night grows frail
The morning light, a gentle kiss
Eases us from night's abyss

In ocean's grip, the day unfolds
While mystery in silence holds
From depths we rise, to greet the morn
In velvet cloak, new worlds are born

With every ray, the darkness flees
Revealing secrets of the seas
A timeless dance, night into day
In inky veil, we make our way

Mariner's Mirage

Upon the sea so vast and wide,
Waves whisper secrets, cannot hide.
A mariner drifts beneath the sky,
Dreams of shores that seem to fly.

Horizon blurs in salt-tinged air,
Mirages dance, surreal and fair.
Stars map journeys to unknown,
Sailor's heart, forever shown.

Storms may rage, yet mind stays clear,
Charting paths through tides of fear.
North Star guides with steady light,
Through endless dark, the soul's delight.

Echoes from the deep arise,
Songs of sea, in lullabies.
Mystic realms within the foam,
Promise mariner a home.

Anchored hope, unwavering gaze,
Through the cataclysmic haze.
Mirage may shift, yet hearth remains,
Where ocean's voice forever reigns.

Veins of Neptune

Through veins of Neptune's deepest blue,
Currents surge in rhythmic cue.
Tales of old in bubbles rise,
Ancient whispers under skies.

Maritime pathways intertwine,
Etched in time, a sacred line.
Beyond the reef, where shadows play,
Mysteries of night and day.

In silence, ocean's pulse revealed,
A heartbeat, ever concealed.
Neptune's veins in patterns vast,
Weave the future, bind the past.

Creatures dance in ebb and flow,
In watery realms, they come and go.
Tameless life in colors bold,
Secrets in their dances told.

Depths unfathomed, worlds unseen,
In liquid realms where dreams convene.
Tranquil tides and tempests both,
In Neptune's veins, the cosmic troth.

Dark Water Melody

Beneath the moon's soft silver sheen,
Whispers twilight's haunting scene.
Dark waters hum a timeless song,
Where boundless echoes drift along.

Ships of dreams on starlit waves,
Sail through ancient, hidden caves.
Melodies in shadows trace,
Mysteries in the ocean's face.

Ghostly chords from depths arise,
In the midnight's shadowed skies.
Mermaids sing with voices pure,
Dark water's call, a sweet allure.

Enchanted strands of twilight's lace,
Weave the night's celestial grace.
Harmony in every swell,
Where dreams and ocean spirits dwell.

Lost mariners in search of dawn,
Find solace as the night moves on.
Dark waters, hold their spectral rhyme,
Through boundless waves, beyond all time.

Beyond the Coral

Where coral limbs embrace the sea,
Lies a realm where spirits flee.
Gardens bloom in colors bright,
Beneath the waves, out of sight.

Ancient reefs stand sentry bold,
Guarding secrets, tales untold.
Fish with scales like jewels gleam,
In the ocean's vivid dream.

Currents weave a silent spell,
In coral's maze where echoes dwell.
Sunlight dances, shadows play,
In this hidden world by day.

Sorrows cast into the deep,
In coral keeps, forever sleep.
Beauty in the silent sweep,
Of ocean's breath, their vigil keep.

Beyond the coral, dreams reside,
In the ebbing, flowing tide.
A world untouched by time's cold hand,
In ocean's heart, a timeless land.

Riddles of the Blue

In oceans deep where secrets glow,
A mystery wrapped in azure flow.
The currents sing a song so true,
Endless echoes, riddles of the blue.

Beneath the waves where shadows play,
Hidden realms in whispered sway.
The fathoms hold a sapphire hue,
Unveiling truths, riddles of the blue.

In twilight's touch, a gentle breeze,
The sea unveils its ancient keys.
A tale untold, both old and new,
In secret depths, riddles of the blue.

Echoing Void

In silent spaces, whispers drift,
A void where echoes gently lift.
A shadow's dance, both wave and tide,
In echoing void, where dreams reside.

The void extends, an endless night,
A canvas dark, devoid of light.
Yet deep within, a lullaby,
In echoing void, where soft dreams lie.

An unseen hand, a silent call,
Resonant whispers, they enthrall.
A mystic chant that glides and glides,
In echoing void, where hope abides.

Whispers Beneath the Waves

Beneath the waves, where silence reigns,
The ocean's voice in soft refrains.
Whispers travel, secrets save,
Mystic murmurs beneath the waves.

The moonlight bathes the ocean's crest,
Nighttime's whispers will attest.
A lullaby that water craves,
Gentle tales beneath the waves.

In the deep where light is sparse,
Voices weave a tranquil arc.
Melodies that subtly brave,
Faint echoes beneath the waves.

Abyssal Dreams

In chasms deep where shadows fall,
Abyssal dreams in silent call.
A world below, where phantoms gleam,
In sullen dark, an endless dream.

The silence speaks in whispered tones,
A somber song in undertones.
Enshrouded mists that softly stream,
In hidden depths, abyssal dream.

There lies a land where darkness blooms,
In silent halls and shadowed rooms.
A twilight realm, where stars redeem,
In hush profound, abyssal dream.

Hidden Horizons

Between the veil of dawn and night,
Where shadows whisper, wanes the light,
A dreamscape dances, soft and free,
Revealing secrets meant to be.

In whispers of the twilight's gaze,
Are hidden paths in twilight's haze,
A realm where stories softly lie,
And every secret bids goodbye.

Horizons hide in hues of blue,
Where ancient tales are born anew,
With every turn, a new surprise,
Beneath the ever-changing skies.

What mysteries lie just beyond,
Through veils of mist, so deep and fond,
A journey waits in silent sleep,
Where dreams and shadows softly creep.

In twilight's arms, we'll fade, we'll soar,
Through hidden realms of evermore,
Discovering what lies untold,
As secrets of the night unfold.

Marine Dusk

As sunlight fades beneath the sea,
The ocean whispers secrets free,
The sky ignites in hues of flame,
As dusk descends to stake its claim.

Waves dance with twilight's gentle kiss,
A symphony of gloaming bliss,
The stars awake, begin to gleam,
Illuminating night's soft dream.

Beneath the waves, the world below,
Awakens in the evening's glow,
As creatures of the deep arise,
To dance beneath the moonlit skies.

The tide retreats with silent grace,
Leaving trails of starfish lace,
In twilight's realm, we wander free,
And in this dusk, forever be.

In marine dusk, we find our place,
A tranquil world of endless space,
Where night and ocean softly blend,
And time itself begins to bend.

Ocean's Lullaby

Beneath the moon's soft silken sigh,
The ocean sings its lullaby,
A song of waves and whispered dreams,
In twilight's tender, silver gleams.

The tides, they ebb with lulling grace,
A soothing rhythm, soft embrace,
In coral beds and shell-lined shores,
The ocean's song forever pours.

Each note a whisper of the sea,
A melody of vast decree,
The gentle splash of moonlit waves,
A harmony the night behaves.

Stars reflect on waters deep,
As ocean cradles us to sleep,
In dreams where mermaids softly cry,
The echoes of a lullaby.

Within this tranquil, ocean's song,
We find a place where we belong,
To dream, to drift, to softly sigh,
In arms of ocean's lullaby.

Phantom Waters

In realms where shadows softly play,
The phantom waters find their way,
Through hidden coves and silent streams,
They carry forth forgotten dreams.

A place where mist and moonlight meld,
Where secrets of the night are held,
In whispers faint, they softly glide,
Through waters deep, where phantoms hide.

Their currents speak in ghostly tones,
Of ancient ships and sunken bones,
A spectral dance beneath the waves,
In haunted depths of ocean graves.

With every crest, a story told,
Of mysteries in waters cold,
Of sailors lost and moonlit nights,
In phantom waters' eerie lights.

In ghostly tides, they find their rest,
These waters of the ocean's quest,
A spectral serenade of yore,
In phantom depths forevermore.

Submerged in Starlight

Beneath the midnight's velvet gaze,
Where constellations weave their maze,
In liquid night, where stars reside,
The cosmos and the seas collide.

Moonbeams dance on cresting waves,
While shadows guard the ocean caves.
Ethereal whispers grace the ear,
As dreams entwine with starlit fear.

Through waters, dark with astral light,
We drift in silence, pure delight.
Celestial tides guide our descent,
Into realms where the heavens are spent.

Beneath the twilight's tender kiss,
The ocean reveals its starlit bliss.
An endless night, both firm and deep,
Where galaxies in silence sleep.

In the abyss where light is born,
The fabric of space-time is torn.
Submerged in starlight, souls take flight,
Eternal wonder in the night.

Abyssal Enigma

In depths where light dares not to gleam,
The silence breeds a quiet dream.
Mysteries wrapped in shadows lie,
Beneath an ever-watchful sky.

Beneath the crush of ocean's weight,
In darkened folds where secrets wait,
A world unknown to mortal eyes,
Where ancient echoes breathe and rise.

The current's sigh, a mournful song,
Guides us where the unknown belongs.
Through labyrinths of coral bone,
Where abyssal creatures make their home.

Onyx tendrils brush our skin,
Inviting us to worlds within.
A symphony that spirits sing,
In ocean depths where mysteries cling.

To question all, yet answer none,
In realms where shadowed dreams are spun.
The abyss extends its coldest hand,
An enigma vast, where we stand.

Ink-Dark Waters

In waters inked with midnight's glow,
Where whispered winds of Neptune blow,
A world beneath the cresting tide,
Calls to us from its darkened side.

Whales' songs drift through marbled black,
Tracing stories, lost the track.
Dancers in the sunken deep,
Luminous secrets they do keep.

Nautilus and glowing eel,
In silent waves of night they feel.
Their bioluminescent light,
Illuminates the endless night.

Currents weave a velvet shroud,
Where dreams and nightmares are allowed.
From shadowed depths, reflections rise,
Mirrored moons in ocean eyes.

Ink-dark waters pull us near,
A siren's call we long to hear,
What lies below the inky veil?
A whispered legend, a mournful tale.

Eternal Deepness

In the chasm of the midnight sea,
Lies a depth of eternity.
Where time itself dissolves away,
In silent depths, where shadows play.

The ocean's heart beats slow and sure,
Its pulse a rhythm, deep and pure.
From canyon's maw to mountain's crest,
Eternal quiet offers rest.

Beneath the layers of the past,
A universe both wide and vast.
Ancient echoes touch the soul,
Whispers of a world made whole.

As sunlight fades to twilight's call,
The deepness echoes, endless, tall.
A space where silence's song is sung,
In tongues of age, forever young.

Our spirits blend with ocean's hue,
In colors deep and ever true.
Eternal deepness holds the key,
To boundless worlds and mystery.

Flow of the Abyss

In the deep where shadows swim,
Silent whispers softly brim.
Currents carve a liquid trail,
Mysteries shrouded in a veil.

Stars above, the ocean's quest,
Unseen wonders never rest.
Echoes of forgotten lore,
Reaching out from ocean's core.

Darkness wraps a velvet glove,
Embracing depths, a silent shove.
Ancient seashells mark the path,
Silent sentinels of wrath.

Seaweed sways with eerie grace,
Ghostly figures find their place.
Echoing the abyssal song,
Where the twilight creeps along.

In the vastness, secrets grow,
Timeless waves that ebb and flow.
Otherworldly spirits kiss,
In the heart of the abyss.

Enchanted Coral Cathedrals

Pillars rise from ocean's floor,
Rainbow hues forevermore.
Luminous, the corals gleam,
In a sunlit, vibrant dream.

Underwater palaces stand,
Crafted by nature's own hand.
Brilliant gardens full of life,
Beauty sharp as any knife.

Schools of fish in joyous play,
Dance through arches night and day.
Whispers of the coral night,
Speak of magic out of sight.

Turquoise chambers, vast and proud,
Hold their court beneath the shroud.
Guardians of the azure realm,
Nature's marvels at the helm.

From these halls of mystic blue,
Life breathes fresh and new.
Sacred, silent, eternal trust,
In the coral's vibrant crust.

Realm of the Endless Blue

An expanse of boundless sky,
Mirrored in the sea's own eye.
Waves that gently kiss the shore,
Whispers of the ocean's lore.

In this realm where dreams take wing,
Oceans to the heavens cling.
Beneath the azure canopy,
Imagination wanders free.

Vast horizons stretch afar,
Guided by a distant star.
Serenade of the tidal crest,
Lays the weary heart to rest.

Emerald tones in waters deep,
Guard the secrets they do keep.
Boundless blue, forever true,
Nurturing both old and new.

Eternal ties to sky and sea,
In this space where spirits flee.
Journey to the edges bright,
In the blue, find endless light.

Where Mermaids Sing

On moonlit waves, their voices rise,
Melodies beneath the skies.
Sirens call with songs so sweet,
Charmed waters 'neath their fleeting feet.

Tales of love and loss they weave,
In the currents, hearts deceive.
Odes to sailors, lost at sea,
Echo through eternity.

Bronze and silver scales they wear,
Caught in threads of salt-kissed hair.
Eyes that speak of ancient rites,
Guard the secrets of their nights.

Underneath the starry veil,
Legends breathe in whispered tale.
To the rhythm of the deep,
Promising a dreamlike sleep.

In the realms where songs take flight,
Carried by the ocean's might,
Mermaids craft their timeless tune,
Beneath the orb of silver moon.

Aquatic Midnight

In the silent heart of night,
Where the ocean meets the stars,
Whispers dance in silvered light,
Echoes of the near and far.

Mystic waves in darkness speak,
Tales of depths so cold and deep,
Where the moonlight softly leaks,
Secrets in the shadows seep.

Coral castles, ghostly bright,
Guard the dreams of slumbered fish,
Midnight's hand a gentle might,
Granting every sunken wish.

Tides of twilight softly sway,
Carrying the weight of time,
In the dusk, no more the day,
Silent as the chimes.

In this world of liquid dark,
Life moves with a hush profound,
Every splash a fleeting spark,
In the night's expansive sound.

Echoes in the Abyss

Deep below where sunlight fails,
Whispers of the ancient sea,
Murmur through the quiet veils,
Tales of what will never be.

Shadows drift in silent streams,
Beneath the waves so cruel,
Memories of forgotten dreams,
In the abyss, they rule.

Echoes of the olden days,
Carved in coral, etched in sand,
Silent hymns in mournful praise,
To a lost and distant land.

Phantom lights beneath the blue,
Glimmer in the void's embrace,
Trace the paths where once they flew,
In the endless, timeless space.

In the depths where time stands still,
Echoes linger, whisper low,
Abyssal songs the darkness fills,
With the tales of long ago.

Twilight Currents

Beneath the dying sun's last glow,
Currents twist and softly blend,
Where the twilight waters flow,
Sun and sea in twilight mend.

Fractured light upon the waves,
Glistens in the fading day,
In the depths, the shadow saves,
Memories in soft array.

Gentle pull and mighty push,
Tides that whisper, currents hum,
In the twilight's tender hush,
Songs of night are softly strum.

Moonrise in the rippling sea,
Sky and water intertwine,
Currents wild and currents free,
Guiding hands in soft incline.

In the tender moments' pass,
Day surrenders to the night,
Currents flow in liquid glass,
Twilight's dance, a pure delight.

Tales from the Trench

In the deepest ocean trench,
Where the sunlight fears to tread,
Stories whispered in the drench,
By the shadows, largely led.

Creatures of the abyssal deep,
Graph their tales in silent verse,
Through their endless twilight sleep,
In a world they call the purse.

Mariners have seldom seen,
What the trench has held in trust,
Ancient empires in between,
Silent, silted, turned to dust.

Pearl and jet in unseen light,
Glimpse of life within the gloom,
Ancient spirits of the night,
Guarding secrets of the womb.

Through the pressure, through the cold,
Trench-born life whispers its tale,
Of mysteries yet to unfold,
In the oceans dark and pale.

Nebula of Nautical Dreams

Amongst the waves where the starlight gleams,
Whispers of the ocean weave their silent themes.
Vessels sail through moonlit streams,
In a nebula of nautical dreams.

The tide calls out with a gentle plea,
Embrace the mystique of the boundless sea.
Stars reflect on water, wild and free,
Dancing in cosmic reverie.

Silvery fish weave their ghostly threads,
Tracing the paths where voyagers tread.
Beneath the surface where visions are bred,
Lies a world clothed in stardust, richly spread.

Lost in the depths of time and space,
Mermaids hum with enchanting grace.
In this realm, all fears erase,
With each current's tender embrace.

Amidst coral halls, where secrets lay,
Mariners find rest at the close of day.
In a nebula where dreams softly sway,
Sailors' hopes and wishes play.

Eerie Seamounts

Beneath the sea where shadows creep,
Mountains rise from caverns deep.
Whispers echo, as specters sleep,
On eerie seamounts, secrets keep.

In the dark where no light roves,
Ancient beings find their coves.
The weight of ages silently moves,
Amidst the coral's haunted groves.

Silent sentinels of the deep,
Guardians of dreams that seafarers keep.
Where the darkened waters weep,
Souls lost in time now sleep.

Ghostly lights flicker without heed,
Guiding wanderers in their need.
Through the currents, the shadows lead,
A dance of mystery, unseen, freed.

Eerie seamounts stand alone,
Silent watchers, overgrown.
In their grasp, the sea's breath moan,
Eternal drifters, cast in stone.

Drown in Illumination

Beneath the veil of night's embrace,
The ocean's light begins to chase.
Glowing creatures in their place,
In the depths, we drown in grace.

Bioluminescence bright and wild,
Paints the water, temptress mild.
In this stillness, fate compiled,
Dreams like stardust, undefiled.

With each pulse, the dark unfurls,
Revealing hidden, twinkling pearls.
Life's brief dance in light's swirls,
Silent songs, as water curls.

Silent depths with secrets cast,
Moments fleeting, never last.
In this glow, the present's past,
Eternal now, vast and fast.

Immersed in light, we find our peace,
In the dark, where wonders cease.
Drifting softly, sorrows release,
In the ocean's warm, bright lease.

Abyssal Enchantment

In the deep, where the silence sings,
Mysteries wear their secret rings.
Here, the heart of Neptune brings,
Abyssal enchantment on shadowed wings.

Through the void where darkness reigns,
Life persists in ethereal veins.
Soft and silent, devoid of chains,
In the abyss where wonder remains.

Creatures of the depths glide slow,
In this realm where whispers flow.
Shadows dance in a ghostly show,
Where time is lost, forever to go.

A symphony of the unknown,
Where dreams of mariners find their throne.
In the abyss, where all is thrown,
A realm unseen, yet fully grown.

Abyssal enchantment calls to thee,
To explore the depths and mysteries.
In this world beneath the sea,
Find the magic, just let it be.

Turbulent Blue

Waves clash in roaring swell,
Crash of ocean, tale to tell.
Azure fury, tempest high,
Below the wild, the sea birds cry.

Boats sway in frantic dance,
Under moon's ephemeral glance.
Sailors grip the creaking mast,
Hoping turmoil swiftly passed.

Storm's embrace, a violent song,
Ocean's grip, chaotic, strong.
The sky illuminates with might,
A beacon through the darkest night.

Salt and spray, a fierce embrace,
Turbulent blue, a restless place.
Nature's power, raw and pure,
Through the storm, will we endure?

Calm returns, as daylight breaks,
Quietude from storm awakes.
Turbulent blue fades to serene,
A reminder of the strength unseen.

Deep Sea Echoes

Beneath the waves, a silent hum,
Echoes through the deep and numb.
Secrets whispered slow and low,
In the depths, where few dare go.

Coral cities, vibrant bright,
Hiding under murky light.
Schools of silver dart and gleam,
Silent actors in a dream.

Mysteries in caverns sprawled,
Ancient tales, unanswered called.
Creatures glide in shadow's cast,
Echoes of a hidden past.

Pressure weighs in darkest deep,
Where the secrets never sleep.
In the quiet, whispers play,
Voices of the ocean's sway.

Deep sea echoes call the brave,
To explore the ocean's grave.
In their stories, find our path,
Silent depths with all their wrath.

Nautical Nightfall

Moon adorns the navy sky,
Stars like pearls, they amplify.
Across the sea, night's gentle sway,
Guiding sailors on their way.

Lanterns lit on decks so broad,
Glowing softly, like a nod.
Waves reflect celestial light,
A symphony of silent night.

Whispers ride the cool night air,
Tales of journey, tales of care.
Underneath the cosmic spread,
Dreams and hopes are softly fed.

Nightfall wraps in calming grace,
Ocean's lullaby in place.
Hearts at peace, no fear nor fright,
Soothed by the nautical night.

Horizon's edge, where sea meets sky,
Embrace of night, a gentle sigh.
Till morning's light will break the spell,
Nighttime's tale, in hearts will dwell.

Underwater Silence

In the blue, where light fades slow,
Silence wraps in undertow.
Every echo, soft and sweet,
A tranquil yet profound retreat.

Creatures move in ghostly flight,
Through the beams of dappled light.
Quiet chorales, gently played,
Symphonies in muted shade.

Reefs like castles, standing still,
Homes of life, and nature's will.
Silent meadows of the sea,
Whispers of tranquility.

Bubbles trace a silent route,
In the deep, where world is mute.
Echoes of the ancient song,
In the quiet, we belong.

Silence holds a sacred space,
Underwater, filled with grace.
In the depths, find solace near,
Peace within the stillness clear.

Eternal Blue Mirage

Beyond the azure skies, where dreams take flight,
Veils of endless blue, enchant the night,
Mirages of fantasy, where horizons cry,
Whispers of infinity, in the bold, bright sky.

An oasis of glimmers, where suns reside,
Mirroring the heavens, in vast cosmic tide,
My heart beats steady, beneath celestial sheen,
Lost in the illusion, where time's unseen.

In this painted expanse, where souls entwine,
Hues mix and mingle, in harmony's shrine,
Distant echoes call from realms above,
Singing lullabies of eternal love.

Eternal skies of dreams, where spirits bide,
Chasing shadows, where the mystics guide,
Tranquil is the dance, in this boundless sea,
A mirage of peace, in eternity's decree.

Shadows in the Brine

Deep beneath the waves, where secrets hide,
Whispers from the deep, in shadows glide,
Mysteries unfold, in the ocean's rhyme,
Tales of ages past, lost in brine's embrace.

Currents weave a story, of whispered grace,
Ancient echoes drift, in the endless chase,
In the silent depths, where the shadows play,
Legends come to life, in the sea's soft sway.

Specters of the deep, in stillness lie,
Glimpses of the past, beneath the sigh,
Figures drift in whispers, through the sombre mist,
Bound by unseen chains, in an ocean's tryst.

In the twilight realms, where dreams reside,
Beneath the ocean's kiss, where spirits bide,
A world unfolds, in calm serenity,
Shadows in the brine, an ancient melody.

Wonders of the Undersea Kingdom

In the azure depths, where coral breathe,
A kingdom thrives, in the ocean's sheath,
Gardens bloom, in colors most divine,
A symphony of life, in the briny shrine.

Fish of every hue, in ballet glide,
Jellyfish like lanterns, drift with the tide,
Seahorses prance, in this magic place,
A carnival of wonders, in the ocean's embrace.

Anemones sway in the gentle flow,
Hidden treasures, where the currents go,
Mystical creatures, in the depths dream,
Wonders unspoken, like a silent scream.

In caverns vast, where the sea nymphs sing,
Echoes of beauty, in an endless ring,
In the undersea realms, where dreams unfurl,
The wonders astound, in a sparkling swirl.

Ancient Mariner's Dream

Upon the rolling waves, where legends soar,
An ancient mariner dreams, of distant shore,
Sea winds whisper tales, of yore and might,
Stars guide his journey, through the endless night.

Memories of voyages, etched in mind's eye,
Battles with tempests, under stormy sky,
Lost in reverie, of uncharted seas,
Boundless adventures, in the ocean's breeze.

Oceans of mystery, beneath the moon's beam,
Treasures and perils, in the mariner's dream,
Glimpses of Atlantis, in the midnight blue,
Whispers of mermaids, a mythical crew.

Anchored in twilight, where the past aligns,
The mariner's heart, in distant echoes finds,
In dreams of waters, serene and vast,
An ancient mariner's soul, finds peace at last.

Watery Phantoms

In depths where shadows play,
Soft echoes fill the deep,
Whispers of the night,
Where phantoms gently weep.

Waves, like tender hands,
Caress the ocean's floor,
Secrets long forgotten,
Cut through to the core.

Beneath the moonlit veil,
A dance of light and shade,
Watery phantoms twirl,
Where dreams are gently laid.

The sea, it sings a song,
A lullaby of old,
Haunting every sailor,
In watery whispers bold.

Lost souls and ancient tales,
Swim through the blue abyss,
Eternal in their journey,
In waves of endless bliss.

Depths of Quietude

Silent whispers in the deep,
Where time itself seems still,
A world beneath the waves,
Where shadows softly spill.

In caverns cold and dark,
A peace profound does lay,
The depths of quietude,
Where echoes softly sway.

Ancient and serene,
The ocean's timeless dream,
A cradle of the night,
With stars that softly gleam.

Beneath the murmuring tides,
A world unto its own,
In depths of quietude,
The soul can find its home.

A sanctuary vast,
Where silence roams so free,
In ocean's quiet depths,
The heart finds harmony.

Chasm of Tides

Where oceans rise and fall,
A chasm deep and wide,
The tides, relentless force,
In nature's rhythmic stride.

Waves crash upon the shore,
With whispers of the past,
In chasm of the tides,
Eternity is cast.

The sea, a storyteller,
Of legends old and grand,
In every ebb and flow,
Its secrets shift like sand.

The chasm pulls and tugs,
In dance of moon and sea,
An endless give and take,
Of nature's harmony.

In this eternal play,
Where land and ocean meet,
The chasm of the tides,
Sings ever bittersweet.

Nautical Nights

Beneath a sky of stars,
Where whispers of night play,
Sailors chase the moon,
Across the ocean's sway.

The ship, a ghostly form,
In sea's embrace so tight,
A voyage into dreams,
On these nautical nights.

Winds sing a lullaby,
Through rigging and the sails,
Guiding hearts and secrets,
On twilight's tender trails.

In the silver glow,
Of moon's reflective light,
The sea's a realm of wonder,
In nautical nights so bright.

A serenade of waves,
Cradles slumbering souls,
As stars weave tales of old,
In ocean's gentle shoals.

Mysterious Abyss

In the depths of the endless night,
Creatures dance without daylight,
Shadows ripple, dark and fine,
Whispers echo through the brine.

Hidden realms beneath the waves,
Silent dragons guard their caves,
Luminous ghosts in silent streams,
Haunt the realms of ancient dreams.

Endless sermons of the sea,
Speak in tongues of mystery,
Curved horizons hold their breath,
'Neath the shroud of ocean's depth.

Eerie glows on tranquil sands,
Map a world of distant lands,
Eyes perceive what minds resist,
Secrets of the vast abyss.

Timeless journeys, boundless quest,
Seeker's heart can never rest,
In the veil of water's kiss,
Lies the mystic, dark abyss.

Echoes from the Seafloor

Glimpses of a bygone age,
Written on the ancient page,
Fossil stories etched in stone,
Songs of oceans we've not known.

Coral castles, sunken ships,
Silent harps and weary lips,
Echoes rise from deepest flight,
Tales of creatures lost in night.

Dancing in the azure glow,
Memories of tides that flow,
Whispers of the water's lore,
Ripple through the ocean floor.

Bubbles drift and gently fade,
Veiling secrets, calmly laid,
Curtains of the sea unfurled,
To reveal their hidden world.

In the depths, where silence weighs,
Stories of a thousand days,
Listen close and you may hear,
Echoes from a time unclear.

Veins of the Abyss

Crimson webs in waters cold,
Mysteries of a tale untold,
Twisting, turning, deep they course,
Veins of life, a silent force.

Flowing through the dark expanse,
Brimming with a hidden dance,
Fathoms deep, they weave their art,
Secrets held within their heart.

Unseen paths and silent streams,
Mingle with the ocean's dreams,
Lifeblood of a world unknown,
Veins that whisper and intone.

Coursing through the murky night,
Carrying the spirits' light,
Letters penned in unseen ink,
Binding worlds in every link.

Restless rivers, fluid lines,
Mark the charts of ancient signs,
In the deep's embracing kiss,
Pulse the veins of the abyss.

Cradle of Giants

In the ocean's deep embrace,
Giants move with silent grace,
Timeless beings, ancient might,
Guardians of the endless night.

Slumbering in tranquil peace,
Legends of the deep's release,
Cradle rocked by tidal waltz,
Mythical, without a pulse.

Motion in the boundless reach,
Waves of wisdom, old and each,
Breaths, so vast and slow to trace,
Cradle in this boundless space.

In the shadows 'neath the glow,
Elders of the brine bestow,
Whispers of the cosmic dance,
In their languid, ancient trance.

Giants stir in deep repose,
In the heart where no one goes,
Cradle of a world confined,
Giants of an ageless kind.

Uncharted Depths

Beneath the waves where secrets sleep,
In silence, ancient echoes sweep,
Lost treasures lie in caverns deep,
Where shadows through the waters creep.

With every dive, a world unfolds,
A realm where mystery beholds,
Creatures in their silent strolls,
Guarding tales the ocean holds.

Coral castles, dusky lights,
Weaving through the darkest nights,
In these depths, the deep sea knights,
Keep their secrets out of sight.

Waves above, a dance divine,
Below, the cryptic tales align,
In the murky ocean brine,
Whispers of the past entwine.

Uncharted depths call out to me,
Promising a mystery,
In the ocean's heart, the key,
To timeless, hidden history.

Abyssal Serenade

In the darkness, currents play,
A soft serenade, night and day,
Through the void, their tunes convey,
Gentle notes in black and grey.

Echoes from the deep abyss,
Softly speak of nature's bliss,
In this realm, the shadows kiss,
Silent songs that none dismiss.

Luminescent creatures glide,
Through the vast, the ocean's pride,
Listening to the whispering tide,
In the depths where dreams abide.

Mystic voices softly sing,
Through the void, their echoes ring,
Where the light and darkness cling,
Every note, a secret spring.

Abyssal calls, a haunting tone,
In the deep, the sea's own throne,
Where the soul is not alone,
Listening to the ocean's moan.

Sunken Chronicles

Tales of old beneath the sea,
Locked in sunken memory,
In the depths, forever free,
Lies the ocean's history.

Ruins of a bygone age,
Pages of an ancient page,
In the deep, a lost sage,
Whispers through the ocean's cage.

Ships of yore in silence rest,
Holding secrets in their chest,
In the deep, they are caressed,
By the waves, a gentle guest.

Echoed tales in waters dark,
Leave on history their mark,
In the silence, a hidden park,
Of the sea's eternal arc.

Chronicles of times long lost,
In the ocean's churning frost,
In the waves, they're lightly tossed,
Memories without a cost.

Eclipsed by Tides

Eclipsed by tides, the light falls dim,
A dance of shadows, ocean's hymn,
Where day and night on borders skim,
A twilight realm where dreams swim.

In the lull of waves, a song,
Mysteries that won't belong,
Drifting where the tides grow strong,
Eclipsed shadows glide along.

Moonlit ripples, soft and faint,
In the sea, a shadow's paint,
Whispers of the night restraint,
Mingling with the light's quaint.

Stars reflect on waters' sheen,
A celestial, hushed serene,
In the tides' eternal scene,
Dancing shades of in-between.

Eclipsed rhythms, heartbeat slow,
Where the sea and moonlight flow,
In this twilight's tender glow,
Ocean's secrets softly show.

Lost Cities Below

Below the waves, where secrets lie,
In cities drowned, lost to the eye.
Coral spires reach for the night,
Whispers echo from lost light.

Mosaics gleam in twilight deep,
Ancient guardians eternal keep.
Once bustling streets now overgrown,
Silent halls of ghostly stone.

Ruins sing in muted tones,
Echoes of forgotten homes.
Submerged tales of joy and woe,
In the labyrinths below.

Treasures sleep in sunken chests,
Guarded dreams in tranquil rests.
Mermaid's hymn, a siren's plea,
Lost cities' cryptic melody.

Veil of the Nautilus

In ocean's shroud, the nautilus glides,
Secrets held in spirals wide.
Pearled chambers, silent dreams,
Whispering through azure streams.

Mystic shell, an ancient lore,
Guarding time from distant shore.
Hidden paths within the shell,
Through the veil, where legends dwell.

Cloaked in mystery, it sails,
Through the depths where silence pales.
In its wake, a tale untold,
Veil of wonders, ages old.

Silent voyager, timeless echo,
In the deep where currents flow.
Guard the past, reveal the glow,
Of secrets veiled, long ago.

Whale Song Symphony

Through the deep, a symphony calls,
Majestic giants in ocean halls.
Echoing songs, so rich and free,
Whale's timeless, haunting plea.

Currents carry, notes of grace,
Melodies in endless space.
Harmonies of ancient lore,
Resonate from shore to shore.

Beneath the waves, a concert grand,
Sweeping rhythms through sea and sand.
Songs of joy and sorrows past,
In the ocean's vast expanse.

Whale song symphony, grand and true,
Echoes through the ocean blue.
In the depths and through the night,
A serenade of pure delight.

Echoes of Leviathan

In the shadowed deep, a titan stirs,
Leviathan's call, the ocean purrs.
Silent ripples of ancient might,
Echoes stir in moonlit night.

Colossal form in hidden lair,
Guarding secrets, unaware.
Ocean's keeper, shadowed king,
Whispers of the depths it brings.

Storms may rage above the brine,
Yet calm below the currents' line.
Leviathan's presence, silent reign,
Echoes through the dark domain.

Legends sing of mighty deeds,
By the one who plows the deepest seas.
In the abyss, it guards the throne,
Echoes of the realm unknown.

Lost in the Abyss

In the caverns of the mind
Deep shadows swim and twist
Whispers echo undefined
Lost in the abyss

Unseen currents pull me down
Memories, ghosts that hiss
In the silence they will drown
Lost in the abyss

Past the threshold, dark and wide
Ever shifting, ever missed
Where the deepest fears reside
Lost in the abyss

Voices calling out to me
From the shadows, none persist
In their haunting melody
Lost in the abyss

Seeking light within the dark
Silent cries, I resist
Hope a faint and fleeting spark
Lost in the abyss

Deep Blue Reverie

In a realm where dreams abide
Ocean waves, eternal plea
Whispering of tales untied
Deep blue reverie

Mystic tides, they ebb and flow
Carrying the heart's decree
In the depths where secrets glow
Deep blue reverie

Waves that dance beneath the moon
Melodies of mystery
Cradling a silent tune
Deep blue reverie

Amongst the stars, the ocean's flare
Weaving strands of fantasy
Infinite, the night air's care
Deep blue reverie

Drifting through the azure night
Bound by currents wild and free
Finding solace in the light
Deep blue reverie

Embrace of Depth

In the stillness of the deep
Where the currents gently sweep
Cradled in the ocean's keep
Embrace of depth

Whispers of the ancient sea
Songs of endless mystery
Calling to the soul in me
Embrace of depth

Beneath the waves, the world unknown
Where light and shadow richly shone
Finding peace in depths alone
Embrace of depth

Silent echoes, secrets told
In the waters, stories unfold
Timeless, ageless, tales of old
Embrace of depth

Eyes that pierce the deepening blue
Seeking dreams both old and new
Lost in realms of endless hue
Embrace of depth

Velvet Blue

In the hush of twilight's hue
Sky alight with velvet blue
Stars that whisper secrets true
Velvet blue

Kisses of the night unfold
Dreams a tapestry untold
In the darkened sky, behold
Velvet blue

Gentle waves on moonlit shore
Silent whispers, ancient lore
Drawing me forevermore
Velvet blue

Eyes that mirror endless space
Lost within the night's embrace
In the calming, boundless grace
Velvet blue

Soft as night, the dreams ensue
Underneath the stars that strew
Hearts entwined in twilight's view
Velvet blue

Seafloor Secrets

Beneath the waves, where light is rare,
Life thrives in silence, unaware.
Ancient whispers, currents sing,
In the shadows, mysteries cling.

Coral castles, fathoms deep,
Guard the lore that oceans keep.
Shimmering scales, a fleeting glance,
In the dark, the creatures dance.

Anemones wave in ghostly tide,
Hiding secrets they confide.
Octopi with minds so keen,
In the deep, unseen, serene.

Shipwrecks rest in timeless peace,
Nature's grasp, their stories cease.
Barnacles cling to stories old,
In the abyss, tales are told.

Silent depths, where dreams alight,
Echoes of the endless night.
Seafloor secrets, dark and grand,
Unraveled by life's gentle hand.

Benthos Ballad

In the benthos realm below,
Life unfolds with gentle flow.
Crabs and clams in quiet tryst,
Whispers in the ocean mist.

Seagrass sways with ebb and surge,
Songs of the deep they softly urge.
Distant whales their lullabies,
Echo through the ocean skies.

Starfish crawl on muddy plains,
Mapping out their secret lanes.
Pearls of wisdom, shells that gleam,
Craft the benthos' ancient dream.

Shrimp and eels in hidden lairs,
Navigate through liquid airs.
Sediment, a living tale,
Of the sea's eternal wail.

Beneath the blue, in twilight hue,
Worlds unfurl in every view.
Benthos ballad, sung so low,
In the depths, their stories grow.

Plunge into Twilight

Dive into the twilight zone,
Where mysteries are quietly grown.
In the depths where shadows play,
Creatures dance in soft array.

Bioluminescent sparks ignite,
Painting dreams in endless night.
Jellyfish with glowing trails,
Whispering their ancient tales.

Giant squids with gentle glide,
In the ocean's heart, they hide.
Eerie lights from down below,
Guide the way where secrets flow.

Fathomless and ever dark,
Heroes of the deep embark.
In the twilight, life awakes,
In each movement, wonder takes.

In the still, where time is blurred,
Silent souls are gently stirred.
Plunge into the endless sea,
Find the twilight, wild and free.

Beyond the Buoys

Beyond the buoys, the sea calls out,
Whispers of the waves in doubt.
Distant shores and unknown lands,
Drawn by nature's unseen hands.

Sailing past the edge of light,
Stars above and darkened night.
Compass spins without a guide,
Ocean's heart, so vast and wide.

Currents swift, they pull us near,
To the places we revere.
Lost in dreams and salty air,
In the deep, our hearts laid bare.

Whales and dolphins lead the way,
Through the crests and ocean spray.
Ancient mariners of old,
In their tales, true courage bold.

Beyond the buoys, life unfurls,
Waves that whisper hidden pearls.
Journey forth and hear the sea,
In its depths, our spirits free.

Subaqueous Symphony

In the deep where shadows dwell,
A tune begins from ocean's shell.
Whales' songs weave a haunting cry,
Through currents cold, they signify.

Coral reefs, a vibrant score,
Crustaceans dance on ocean floor.
Anemones with tendrils wide,
Sway gently with the rhythmic tide.

Dolphins leap and twist with grace,
In nature's grand aquatic space.
Clownfish dart through morning's hush,
A cacophony in silent rush.

Angler's lure, a ghostly light,
Guides the chorus, whispers slight.
Sharks glide past in silent sweep,
Guardians of the sunless deep.

Jellyfish pulse, ethereal glow,
Softly chanting as they flow.
Each wave a note, a melody rare,
The ocean's symphony everywhere.

Midwater Mysteries

Beneath blue waves where sun does fade,
Lies a realm of twilight shade.
Creatures glide in silent grace,
Mysteries hide in empty space.

Silver scales in spectral gleam,
Drifting through the haunted stream.
Light refracts in liquid night,
Unfurling secrets out of sight.

Squid with arms like ghostly wraiths,
Dance through water in measured paces.
Bioluminescent truths unfurl,
Lighting the abyss in swirl.

Tentacles of mythic size,
Brush the depths where shadow lies.
Mermaids' whispers swirl and whine,
Lost to time in brine and brine.

Giant shadows, fleeting fast,
Echoes of a distant past.
In midwater, where shadows drift,
Timeless tales in silence lift.

Ephemeral Depths

In fleeting moments, dark and deep,
Neptune's secrets, shadows keep.
Ephemeral whispers in the night,
Beneath the waves, out of sight.

Glimmering fish with scales so bright,
Cut through the ocean, swift in flight.
Fleeting glimpses of unknown forms,
In depths where liquid silence storms.

Seahorses drift, tails entwined,
In delicate dance, space aligned.
Bubbles rise and burst unseen,
Ephemeral dreams in ocean's sheen.

Anemones, soft tendrils spread,
Through waters where old legends tread.
Whales' songs echo, soft and clear,
In mid-depth realms, they disappear.

Crashing waves obscure the light,
Fragile moments, out of sight.
In depths where secrets softly weep,
Lies the magic, dark and deep.

Nautilus Nocturne

Ancient shell in moonlit glow,
Twists and turns with ebb and flow.
Nautilus in ocean's thrall,
Glides through timeless hall.

Midnight realms where shadows play,
Creatures of the night display.
In spirals deep, they find their way,
Through the waters cold and grey.

Silent guardian of the past,
In your coils, secrets cast.
Under star-strewn sky you roam,
Nautilus, your drifting home.

Octopus with tendrils vast,
Midnight shadow, fleeting fast.
Under moon's watchful light,
Creatures weave their dance tonight.

In the deep, a silent tune,
Echoes softly with the moon.
Nautilus in endless flight,
Navigates the sea by night.

Coral Cathedral

In the depths of oceans wide,
Where sunlight dares not to reside,
A cathedral of coral, ever grand,
Waves its spires like a silken hand.

With hues of violet, blue and gold,
Ancient stories it has told,
A sanctuary beneath the sea,
Where life breathes, untamed and free.

Silent arches frame the deep,
Where time and tides in whispers sleep,
A realm where shadows dance and play,
Eternal night, transformed to day.

Fish in reverence do glide,
Through the currents, side by side,
A vibrant choir in liquid light,
Serenades the quiet night.

Beneath the raging storm's appeal,
Lies this sacred, coral steal,
An underwater holy ground,
Where nature's grace is truly found.

Silent Blue Realm

Beyond the reach of man's refrain,
Lies a kingdom vast, arcane,
Silent, endless, blue in hue,
A world of secrets, born anew.

Whales compose a solemn song,
In the silence, echo strong,
Mountains rise from ocean's bed,
In this realm where dreams are fed.

Kelp forests sway in gentle tides,
Sheltering where life resides,
Softly whispering to the night,
In the dark, a glistening light.

Gentle giants travel far,
Guided by a distant star,
From the surface to the brink,
Comes the call, the ocean's link.

Here the pulse of life remains,
Flowing in the ancient veins,
A silent, blue realm, wondrous deep,
Where nature's treasures softly sleep.

Submerged Secrets

Beneath the waves, where shadows play,
Lies a world both night and day,
Guarded by the ocean's might,
A realm that basks in muted light.

Ancient ruins whispered tales,
Lost in time, where memory pales,
Cryptic secrets, waters hide,
Wrapped in currents, oceans wide.

Relics of forgotten lands,
Rest within the seabed sands,
Etched in stone and coral tomb,
Stories bloom where silence looms.

Mermaids weave their mystic lore,
In the currents evermore,
Legends of a time gone by,
In the deep, where echoes lie.

Submerged secrets, held so tight,
In the vast aquatic night,
Veils of water, stories keep,
In the ocean's heart, they sleep.

Mariner's Lament

Across the waves, a mariner sighs,
Beneath the canopy of skies,
Lost to the rolling ocean's swell,
He carries tales too deep to tell.

A mast that creaks in winds lament,
A soul adrift, with heart's content,
Stars, his guide across the deep,
In the night, his secrets keep.

A lover's voice, a distant shore,
Echoes of a time before,
Waves that sing a mournful tune,
Beneath the pale, betraying moon.

Salt-stained hands and weathered eyes,
In the tempest, truth belies,
Memories etched in water's flow,
Sailor's heart, the sea does know.

Mariner's lament, so softly told,
In whispered winds, the tales unfold,
Ocean's call, a siren's plea,
Silent now, eternally.

Nautical Enigma

Beneath the waves, a secret lies,
In depths that shimmer, dark and wise,
The ocean whispers soft and low,
Of mysteries only currents know.

A sail unfurls to unknown lands,
With winds that guide and stars command,
The sea's enigma calls my name,
In whispers, shadows, endless same.

A compass lost in time's embrace,
Navigates this liquid space,
Yet every dot and every line,
Hides secrets of the deep, divine.

The moon's reflection dances free,
Upon the enigmatic sea,
Revealing hints, yet keeping more,
Locked within its shifting floor.

To voyage forth with courage bold,
Unravel tales the currents told,
For in the depths where darkness clings,
Lie the secrets of forgotten things.

Sunken Twilight

The twilight sinks beneath the sea,
With hues of gold and mystery,
The evening dives to ocean's deep,
Where silent currents gently seep.

Beneath the waves, where shadows drift,
A realm of wonder, darkly gift,
Corals glow in muted light,
In realms that mark the fall of night.

Sunsets swallowed by the tide,
Into the deep they gently slide,
To rest within the ocean's hold,
Where timeless tales of dusk unfold.

The sky and sea in twilight blend,
As day and night to ocean send,
A farewell kiss, a whispered dream,
To drift upon the midnight stream.

Deep in the twilight, secrets gleam,
Like stars within a watery dream,
And in the sunken realms below,
Lies the twilight's final glow.

Forgotten Depths

Beneath the surface, shadows play,
In realms where light has lost its way,
Where ancient echoes softly sleep,
In the embrace of oceans deep.

Forgotten depths, where secrets dwell,
In silken waves and silent swell,
Here time stands still, as shadows weave,
A tapestry none can perceive.

Lost relics of the past remain,
In underwater dark domain,
Their stories buried, songs unsung,
By coral whispers gently sprung.

In crevices where shadows hide,
The currents sweep in steady stride,
Guardians of secrets kept,
In the depths where legends slept.

Yet from these depths, a silent call,
Echoes through the ocean's hall,
Of mysteries the sea has kept,
In forgotten depths where secrets crept.

Eclipsed by Blue

Beneath a sky of endless hue,
The world above is lost from view,
An azure cloak, a seamless blend,
In waters where the echoes bend.

An eclipse of blue, where light is veiled,
In ocean depths where dreams have sailed,
A hidden realm begins anew,
Where day and night in blue construe.

Beneath the waves, a silent world,
In liquid depths, the truth unfurled,
Where time dissolves to endless flow,
And shadows dance in undertow.

Eclipsed by blue, the surface fades,
To realms where quiet sunlight wades,
Through prisms deep and stories spun,
In currents where the echoes run.

Through cerulean dreams I drift,
In silence where the waters lift,
An ocean world in endless blue,
Eclipsed where secrets wander through.

Undercurrents of Time

Beneath the surface, whispers flow,
Currents of time, where secrets go.
Eternity's pull, silent and deep,
In the ocean's heart, memories keep.

Waves dance to a timeless song,
Cradling echoes that forever belong.
Infinite tides, shifting with grace,
Washing the past without a trace.

Hidden below, in darkness they hide,
Moments and dreams, adrift in the tide.
Seasons of life, carried away,
In undercurrents, they silently sway.

Whispers of love, tales of woe,
In the deep currents, they sow.
Ebbing and flowing, never to cease,
Time's secret keeper, in eternal peace.

Journey through depths, and you'll find,
Traces of stories left behind.
In the ocean's embrace, timeless and wide,
Undercurrents of time, forever abide.

Depths of Serenity

In the ocean's calm, we find release,
A tranquil world of endless peace.
Waves murmur soft, in a soothing breath,
Cradling life, in the quietest depth.

Blue horizons, stretching far,
Underneath, where wonders are.
Harmony reigns, in the depth below,
Serenity's touch in gentle flow.

Whales sing their ancient song,
To the deep, they all belong.
In the stillness, a world serene,
Colors vibrant, luminescence keen.

Coral gardens, in vibrant array,
Beneath the waves, where sunrays play.
Life in balance, in peaceful choir,
A realm of peace to inspire.

Dive deep within, leave cares behind,
In the ocean's heart, peace you'll find.
Depths of serenity, calling us near,
In the quiet deep, nothing to fear.

The Midnight Zone

In the light's retreat, where darkness reigns,
Mysteries dwell in the ocean's veins.
Creatures of night, where shadows dance,
In the midnight zone, life takes a chance.

No sun to guide, no dawn to see,
Eerie beauty in the darkened sea.
Luminescent sparks, a fleeting glow,
In the midnight realm, soft and slow.

Abyssal plains, in silence vast,
Echoes of the ancient past.
Adapting to the endless night,
Survivors thrive without the light.

Creatures strange, with unseen eyes,
Navigating where darkness lies.
Bioluminescent whispers blend,
In the midnight zone, mysteries send.

Where pressure mounts and light refrains,
Life persists in secret chains.
The midnight zone, profound and deep,
Guarding secrets in its silent keep.

Guardians of Atlantis

Beneath the waves, a city sleeps,
Hidden where the ocean weeps.
Guardians stand, in quiet might,
In Atlantis's depths, out of sight.

Statues grand of ancient lore,
Protecting secrets evermore.
Marble halls and towers tall,
In the silent depths, they call.

Legends whisper through the tide,
Stories of the lost they bide.
Guardians watch with stoic grace,
In Atlantis's long-lost embrace.

Waters deep, their eternal cloak,
Veiling wonders as they spoke.
Silent sentinels of the sea,
Witness to what once would be.

In sacred watch, they keep the peace,
Hoping time's grip will release.
Guardians of Atlantis, strong,
Holding back the past so long.

Whispers Beneath Waves

In the silent ocean's deep array,
Where moonlight dares to strand,
Whispers weave through soft ballet,
Across the hidden sand.

Fishes glide in gentle arcs,
Through waters calm and clear,
While ancient songs in twilight marks,
The tales we scarcely hear.

Shells do hold the murmured past,
Of sailors' dreams and fears,
In every crevice, shadows cast,
Echoes of yesteryears.

Bubbles rise in mystic dance,
Toward the azure sky,
From where the secrets of romance,
In soft acoustics lie.

The ocean's heartbeats slowly fade,
Yet whispers still remain,
Beneath the waves where dreams cascade,
In a soft and endless chain.

Sunken Secrets

Beneath the green and murky veil,
Lies treasure yet unseen,
In whispered depths where shadows dwell,
A kingdom's sunken sheen.

Coral-grown and lost to time,
A city once so grand,
Now slumbers in the ocean's rhyme,
Beneath a bed of sand.

Artifacts from ages past,
Enshrouded, mute and still,
In cryptic forms they've been recast,
By nature's quiet will.

Seaweed curls in silent grace,
Around forgotten stones,
Guardians of this ancient place,
Where history's breath intones.

Mariners that seek the deep,
In search of fables old,
Will find the secrets oceans keep,
In stories subtly told.

Haunted Blue Depths

In the heart of the ocean's blue,
Where sunlight fades from sight,
Ghostly echoes murmur through,
The everlasting night.

Phantoms glide through watery veils,
In silence, hush and cold,
Their tales are told in secret trails,
Of mysteries untold.

Sunken ships in eerie sleep,
With hulls of crumbling rust,
In haunted depths their secrets keep,
Shrouded in ancient dust.

Specters of the mariners lost,
In depths where shadows creep,
Are bound forever by the cost,
Of promises they keep.

Moonlit currents softly trace,
The paths of spirits' roam,
In haunted depths, in hidden place,
Far from their earthly home.

Twilight Currents

As daylight fades, the currents glow,
    With twilight softly bright,
In waves where tender breezes blow,
    Beneath the coming night.

The sea's vast heart begins to shine,
    With hues of dusky dream,
In twilight's cloak, the stars align,
    And dance in ocean's seam.

Beneath the surface, shadows blend,
    In rippled low refrain,
The currents twist, the shadows bend,
    To twilight's soft terrain.

    In this calm and gentle time,
    The waters sing their song,
    A melody in fluent rhyme,
    Where twilight streams belong.

The ocean's breath in tranquil sighs,
Through night's embrace does sweep,
    A lullaby beneath the skies,
    That leads the world to sleep.

Legend of the Kraken

In the depths of ocean's lore,
A giant stirs beneath the waves.
Ancient whispers speak of yore,
Where sailors met their watery graves.

Tentacles reach far and wide,
A shadow dark as midnight's hue.
Stories spread both far and side,
Of terror from the deepest blue.

Eyes that gleam with emerald light,
Guarding secrets never known.
In the silence of the night,
The Kraken claims his fearsome throne.

Waves crash with mighty roar,
Echoes of a timeless fight.
For those who dared to seek the core,
Met with fate's unyielding might.

In mariner's songs, the echo stays,
A legend whispered on the breeze.
The Kraken's tale, through endless days,
A mystery beneath the seas.

Embrace of the Seafloor

Below the tides where sunlight fades,
A world of shadows comes alive.
Where every secret's softly laid,
In hidden shelters, creatures thrive.

Corals dance with gentle grace,
In currents' tender, caressing arms.
Each crevice holds an ancient face,
In this domain of subtle charms.

Whispers through the ocean flow,
Mysteries in the silent deep.
Life in gentle ebb and grow,
In the seafloor's cool embrace, they sleep.

Here the ceaseless rhythms play,
A symphony of waves and stone.
In this realm both night and day,
The seafloor sings a song its own.

Beneath the waves where dreams are born,
In tranquil hush, the world explores.
The seafloor's love is deeply sworn,
To cradle life forevermore.

Blue Void

In realms of sapphire and cobalt hue,
A vast expanse so endless, wide.
The ocean's depths, the deepest blue,
Where secrets in the shadows hide.

The surface sparkles in daylight's kiss,
Yet underneath, a silent void.
A realm of wonder, of endless bliss,
Where cosmic darkness is deployed.

Creatures of the dark abyss,
Glide through fields of liquid night.
In whispers, speak the ocean's wish,
To keep its mysteries out of sight.

Diving through the azure haze,
Where light and darkness intertwine.
The blue void sings in mellow phase,
A song of love and brine.

Eternal blue, an endless dream,
An ocean vast and free.
In the void where silence gleams,
We find our place to be.

Ephemeral Tides

The tides that kiss the sandy shore,
Are fleeting moments, never still.
Ephemeral as waves in lore,
They dance to time's perpetual will.

Morning's light, they gently rise,
In silver gleam of dawn anew.
Whispering beneath the skies,
Faint echoes of the ocean's view.

By midday sun, they swell and peak,
A harmony of crest and trough.
In this rhythm, life they seek,
Constant flow and soft rebuff.

Twilight brings the tide's retreat,
A soft descent to tranquil plains.
Quietly, the night they greet,
Washing over starlit stains.

In their endless ebb and flow,
The tides remind us, soft and clear.
Life is but a passing show,
Each moment precious, fleeting, dear.

Tales of Sunken Ships

Beneath the waves, where shadows play,
Ancient mariners silently lay.
Forgotten tales at ocean's floor,
And ghostly whispers evermore.

Shipwrecks tell of tempest's might,
Of distant lands and moons at night.
Barnacles claim the wooden bones,
Of ventures past, marked by stones.

Lost to depths, with treasures hold,
Emerald shrouds and coins of gold.
Mystery dwells in seabed crypts,
In lost, eternal, sunken ships.

Seahorses guard these silent graves,
In cascading, azure waves.
Time stands still in briny frost,
Preserving tales of long lost.

Swallowed dreams and sunken lore,
Lie deeper than the ocean's roar.
In the haunted, blue abyss,
We hear their call, a ghostly kiss.

Heart of the Trench

Deep beneath where light can't reach,
Life survives on darkened beach.
In the chasms of the sea,
Mysteries pulse eternally.

Strange creatures move in spectral light,
In shadows cast by endless night.
Eyes that glow and fangs so white,
In trenches' heart, out of sight.

Pressures crush and silence reigns,
In liquid tombs and hidden veins.
Where fragile life does barely creep,
In the abyss where secrets sleep.

Unknown worlds breathe cold and slow,
In depths where few dare to go.
Secrets of the earth's own lace,
In trench's heart, a hidden place.

From darkness springs a vibrant pulse,
Life that thrives in silent gulphs.
Mariners lost to crushing bench,
Rest eternal in heart of trench.

Midnight Blue Horizon

The sky meets sea in dark embrace,
A midnight blue, an endless space.
Waves lap shores in gentle glide,
Kissing night's vast, misty tide.

Stars reflected in ocean's glaze,
Lighting paths in night's deep haze.
Sailors dream of lands to see,
On the horizon's mystery.

Moonlight dances on dark crests,
Lulling hearts with whispered rests.
In the vastness, dreams take flight,
Guided by the silver light.

Whispers of the night's soft wind,
Speak of worlds where dreams begin.
Horizons blend with shadow's line,
A melding where the night does shine.

In the quiet of the night,
Oceans pave with stars so bright.
Echoes of the day's refrain,
Midnight blue, we meet again.

Cryptic Coral Reefs

Beneath the sparkling, azure seas,
Lie coral reefs with mysteries.
Rainbow labyrinths of life,
In colors and forms so rife.

Hidden nooks and caverns deep,
Where secrets of the ocean sleep.
Fish in hues of lavender blaze,
Dance in corals' cryptic maze.

Anemones with tendrils bright,
Sway in waters, soft twilight.
Octopi in shadows hide,
In crypts where lost dreams bide.

Silent guardians of blue,
Hold secrets old and new.
In coral castles, stories spin,
Tales of places where life begin.

Unwritten legends cling to reefs,
In depths where sunlight briefly weaves.
Eternal guardians, living tombs,
Coral reefs, where life resumes.

Drift Through Darkness

In shadows deep, where whispers lie,
The stars above cast silent sighs,
A moonlit path of silver thread,
Guides the lost, the dreams unsaid.

Ghosts of time in twilight fold,
Gently weave their tales of old,
Through the veil of midnight hue,
In this dark, the light feels true.

Winds that carry echoes still,
Wrap the night in velvet chill,
Silent secrets softly blend,
Till darkness finds its gentle end.

An owl's call in distant pine,
Answers whispers intertwined,
In the heart of night's embrace,
Lost souls find their sacred place.

Stars will fade as dawn ascends,
Night's dark journey finds its end,
Drifting through the shadows' rhyme,
To the edge of morning's chime.

Below the Surface

Beneath the waves where silence keeps,
A world of dreams in mystic sleep,
Hidden realms where shadows play,
In liquid night and crystal day.

Whispers of the ocean's breath,
Echo through the depths beneath,
Silent songs in currents flow,
Stories of a world below.

Coral castles, hidden, bright,
Glow with pure, unearthly light,
Creatures weave through liquid blue,
In this world, forever new.

Depths reveal their secrets rare,
Rich with life, beyond compare,
Mysteries in silent grace,
In the deep's engulfing space.

In this realm of water's guise,
Truths are seen with unseen eyes,
Below the surface, shadows blend,
To an endless ocean's end.

In the Depths of Silence

In the quiet, where time bends thin,
Silence speaks the truth within,
Echoes rest on wings of air,
Whispered words, without a care.

Vast expanse, where silence reigns,
Light and dark, their thin remains,
In the void where whispers cease,
Find the space of gentle peace.

Nature's lullaby, soft and still,
Holds the night in tranquil thrill,
Stars and shadows intertwine,
Weave a tale of the divine.

Soft the world in silence glows,
Through the depths where quiet flows,
A realm apart from noise and din,
In the silence, truths begin.

Deeper yet, in stillness found,
Heartbeats echo, soft, profound,
In the depths where silence lays,
One finds solace in its gaze.

Subaqueous Visions

In the cradle of the deep,
Where ancient secrets gently sleep,
Visions rise from waters dark,
Lit by nature's subtle spark.

Through the sapphire, shadows drift,
In the depths where lights uplift,
Phantom figures, dances weave,
In the ocean's quiet eve.

Coral gardens, hidden dreams,
Glow with soft, enchanting gleams,
Through the ripples, gently glide,
Visions from the ocean's tide.

Beneath the waves, a silence hums,
In this realm where light becomes,
Faint and rare, a distant flame,
Fed by whispers of the same.

Dreams unfold in watery hold,
Tales of depths forever told,
Subaqueous visions, gently trace,
Mysteries in liquid space.

In this underwater realm, so grand,
Nature whispers, hand in hand,
Visions seen, yet ever rare,
In the ocean's depths, laid bare.